All Across Canada

ELLEN WEISBERG AND KEN YOFFE

Welcome to Canada! Canada is the second largest country in the world, and one of the most beautiful. Located on the continent of North America, it is full of lakes and rivers, mountains and tundra, and many different animals. To its south is the United States of America, and to the north, east, and west are oceans. There are over 32 million people in Canada, from many different backgrounds and cultures.

Three adventurous friends, Wandering Wally, Hiking Holly, and Ambling Andy, will now take you across each of Canada's thirteen provinces and territories. Along the way, you will meet other friends of theirs, each named after the capital city of their province or territory.

Come on a journey with Wandering Wally
and Ambling Andy and Hiking Holly.
All Across Canada, under skies blue or gray,
they see many places and friends on the way.
The capital cities of the places they go
are also the names of the friends that they know.

Wandering Wally

Hiking Holly

Ambling Andy

Wandering Through the West with Wally

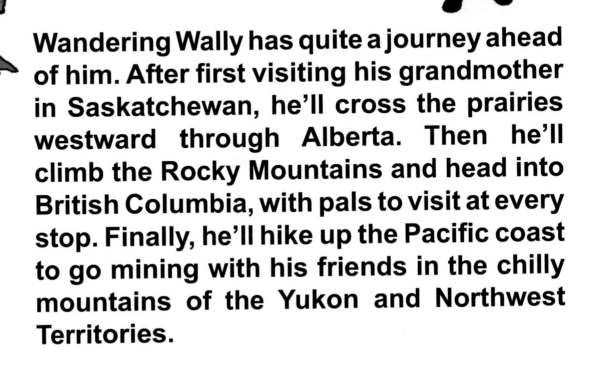

Wandering Wally has quite a journey ahead of him. After first visiting his grandmother in Saskatchewan, he'll cross the prairies westward through Alberta. Then he'll climb the Rocky Mountains and head into British Columbia, with pals to visit at every stop. Finally, he'll hike up the Pacific coast to go mining with his friends in the chilly mountains of the Yukon and Northwest Territories.

Wandering Wally forms a smile
and then begins his quest.
He starts off in the prairies,
and heads off toward the west.
The mountains and the coastline
are places he'll pass through,
with provinces and territories
near the ocean blue.

Wandering Wally

Grandma Regina is named after the capital of Saskat-chewan. More elderly people live here than in any other province. After Wally starts his journey, Grandma Regina decides to do some traveling of her own. Her trip takes her from the town of Saskatoon to the Big Muddy Badlands in the south. The Badlands were actually used as a hideout for outlaws a hundred years ago! The Royal Canadian Mounted Police, or "Mounties," tried to catch these outlaws and put them in jail. The Mounties still make their home in the town of Regina today.

Saskatchewan

Lake Athabasca

Reindeer Lake

•Saskatoon

★•Regina

Big Muddy
Badlands

Grandma
Regina

Regina plans to travel to
the south of Saskatoon.
She tours Big Muddy Badlands,
then goes north to sandy dunes.
With all the many rivers,
and also lakes to cross,
Wally is quite fearful
that Grandma might get lost.

Wally's friend, Edmonton, is named after the capital of Alberta. But Edmonton actually lives in the nearby city of Calgary. Wally makes sure to visit Edmonton in July each year, for that is when he can enjoy the famous Calgary Stampede, the world's largest rodeo! Yet Wally doesn't mind visiting Edmonton during the winter months, as well. "Chinook" winds that come from the Rocky Mountains in wintertime help keep the prairies of southern Alberta warmer than you might expect.

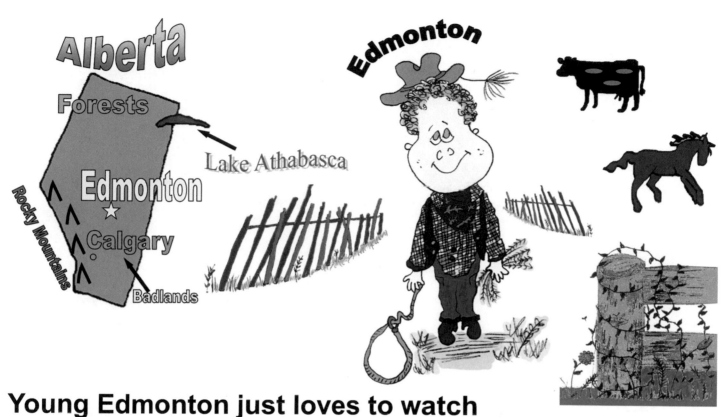

Young Edmonton just loves to watch
the Calgary Stampede.
He helps round up the cattle
and then rides a trusty steed.
He hikes through warming Chinook winds
while heading toward the Rockies,
then walks the southern Badlands,
the forests and the prairies.

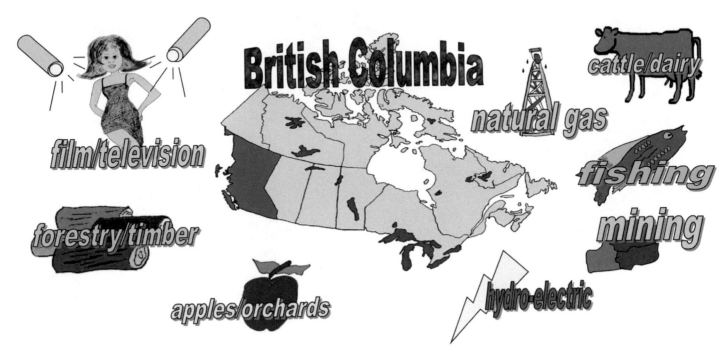

Wally's next visit is to British Columbia, on the west coast of Canada. The parents of his friend, Victoria, had left China to live on Vancouver Island. In fact, British Columbia is home to the largest community of Chinese people in the country. It is also where many movies and television shows are made. Vicky lives near a forest of red cedar, the oldest trees in Canada.

British Columbia

Victoria

On Vancouver Island
there's a lovely
coastal breeze.
Victoria dances round
and round the old
red cedar trees.
To be a famous movie star
is what she often dreams,
while her father catches seafood
in the ocean and the streams.

Next, Wally travels north to Yukon Territory. By now, he is very tired from all of the hiking, and he welcomes the chance to ride his pet, Whitehorse. Whitehorse feels right at home on the Yukon tundra, which is rocky land covered with moss, shrubs, and grasses. Together, Wally and Whitehorse go hunting for Yukon's many precious metals. They also enjoy the beautiful views from Mt. Logan, Canada's highest mountain.

Yukon · Beaufort Sea · Dawson City · Mount Logan · ★Whitehorse · Whitehorse

Whitehorse searches very
hard and tries to find
some gold.
He lumbers very slowly,
and braves the tundra's cold.
For lead and zinc and silver,
he digs and hunts and mines.
Then he catches lots of fish
and happily he dines.

The Northwest Territories are home to Canada's longest river, the Mackenzie. The deepest lake in Canada, Great Slave Lake, is also found here. Wally explores both of these beautiful areas with Yellowknife, an Inuit Indian named after the capital of the Northwest Territories. Wally and Yellowknife have heard that diamonds were discovered in the Ekati and Diavik mines, not far from Yellowknife's home!

Northwest Territories

Banks Island

Inuvik

Victoria Island

Mackenzie River

Great Bear Lake

Mount Nirvana

★ Yellowknife

Great Slave Lake

Yellowknife

Yellowknife works very hard
up in the cold Northwest.
She digs for diamonds all day long
and hardly takes a rest.
She climbs up Mount Nirvana,
with faces very steep.
Then she goes to Great Slave Lake
so wide and cold and deep.

Hiking Around Hudson Bay with Holly

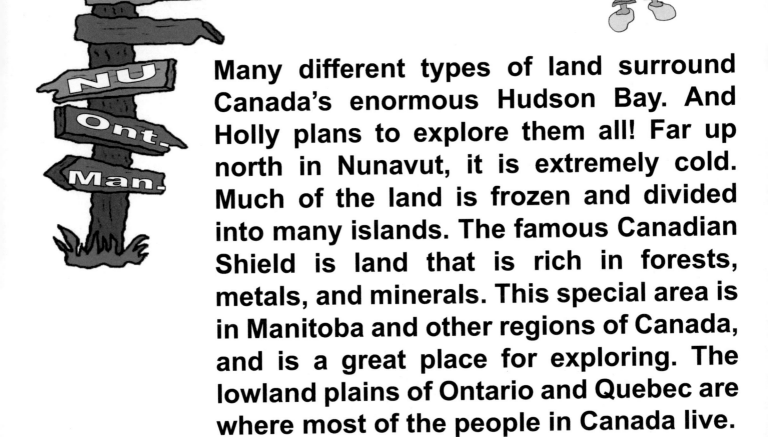

Many different types of land surround Canada's enormous Hudson Bay. And Holly plans to explore them all! Far up north in Nunavut, it is extremely cold. Much of the land is frozen and divided into many islands. The famous Canadian Shield is land that is rich in forests, metals, and minerals. This special area is in Manitoba and other regions of Canada, and is a great place for exploring. The lowland plains of Ontario and Quebec are where most of the people in Canada live.

Holly travels round and round
the lovely Hudson Bay.
The forests and the lowland plains
are where she hikes each day.
She sees big cities in the south
and bison in the fields.
She mines for gold and zinc
and other treasures in the Shield.

Hiking Holly

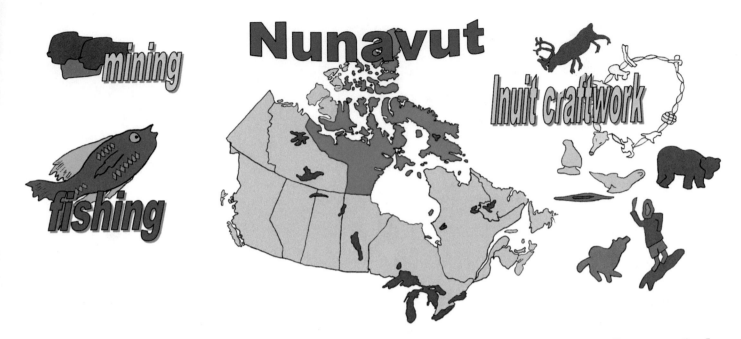

Holly's friend, Iqaluit, is an Inuit who lives in Canada's newest territory, Nunavut. The Inuit are the native people of many parts of Canada. They are very skilled at arts and crafts, such as soapstone sculptures, and they sell their work as a way to make a living. Whenever Holly visits, Iqaluit lends her an extra heavy coat to wear so that she'll stay warm. It gets so cold in Nunavut that ocean, rivers, and lakes freeze, so it is actually hard to tell where the land finishes and the water starts! Amazingly, it is also usually too cold to snow!

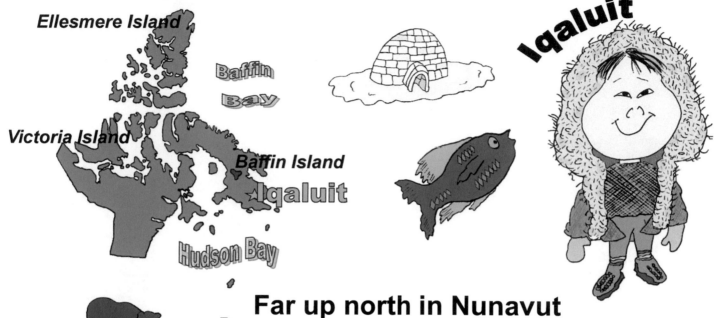

Nunavut

Ellesmere Island

Baffin Bay

Victoria Island

Baffin Island

☆ Iqaluit

Hudson Bay

Iqaluit

Far up north in Nunavut
Iqaluit loves to fish.
It's both his favorite
past-time, as well as
favorite dish.
He walks by frozen
igloos,
and crosses icy lakes,
passing soapstone carvings
that his mother proudly makes.

Holly's next hike is southward around Hudson Bay to the province of Manitoba. Her host, Winnipeg, also called "Winnie" for short, lives on her father's big farm. Winnie's mother works at the Royal Canadian Mint in Manitoba, where she helps make Canadian money. One of Holly's favorite places to visit is Churchill, which has so many polar bear making their dens nearby that it's called the "Polar Bear Capital of the World."

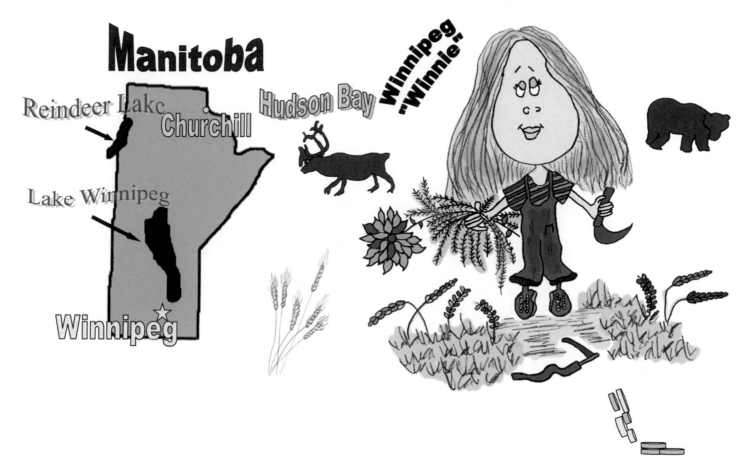

All through Manitoba, Winnie has lots to do.
She travels up to Reindeer Lake, with bears and caribou.
She helps her father harvest wheat and sell it by the pound,
then goes down to the Royal Mint, with coins so bright and round.

vineyards/wine

Ontario

orchards

mining

grain

paper

To the east, Holly greets her friend, Toronto, named after the capital of Ontario. Toronto is also the largest city in all of Canada. More than half of the people in Toronto come from other countries, making it a very interesting place to visit! During Holly's stay, she and Toronto visit Ottawa, which is the capital of the whole country of Canada. Before leaving Ontario, Holly makes sure to visit Niagara Falls, one of the world's most famous waterfalls.

Of Toronto's many neighbors, some are Portuguese.
Others speak Italian; and many speak Chinese.
To Canada's bright capital is where she makes her way.
She heads past Lake Superior and rests in Thunder Bay.

Holly's last hike is to Quebec. Here, she meets her good friend, named after the province's capital, Quebec City. Like most people in the province, Quebec's first language is French, and she teaches Holly a few new words during her stay. They hike through the forests of Quebec, which cover half of the province and make up the most forestland in all of Canada. Quebec and Holly then retreat to the great city of Montreal. It is there that they enjoy many activities, including eating the delicious *Poutine*, a combination of French fries, cheese, and gravy.

Quebec

Hudson Bay

Quebec

Montréal

St. Lawrence River

Quebec

Quebec heads down to
Montreal to see the circus arts.
But comic strips and
Celtic songs are dearest
to her heart.
She likes to dine in restaurants
with French cuisine to eat,
and cheers at all the hockey games
with poutine as a treat.

Ambling Through the Atlantic Provinces with Andy

The Atlantic provinces are on the eastern coast of Canada. Andy is ready to travel through all of them and visit his friends along the way. He and many other tourists will be visiting beautiful places like Prince Edward Island and Nova Scotia, and watching whales dipping in and out of the ocean waters.

The Gulf of St. Lawrence
and Labrador Sea
have lots of great places
for Andy to be.
From Cape Breton Island
he sails on a ship,
passing icebergs and whales
on his seafaring trip.

Ambling Andy

Labrador Sea

NFLD.

Atlantic Ocean

Gulf of
St. Lawrence

P.E.I.

N.B.

N.S.

(United States of America)

Andy's first visit will be with his good friend, Frederic, who lives in New Brunswick. Frederic first takes Andy to Saint John, the oldest city in Canada. Then they travel across the Hartland Bridge, the world's longest covered bridge. A little later on, they go to the Bay of Fundy to watch the highest tides in the world! The two friends take a break from their travels and sit together, eating interesting-looking plants called *fiddleheads*. Frederic tells Andy that fiddleheads are one of New Brunswick's favorite dishes.

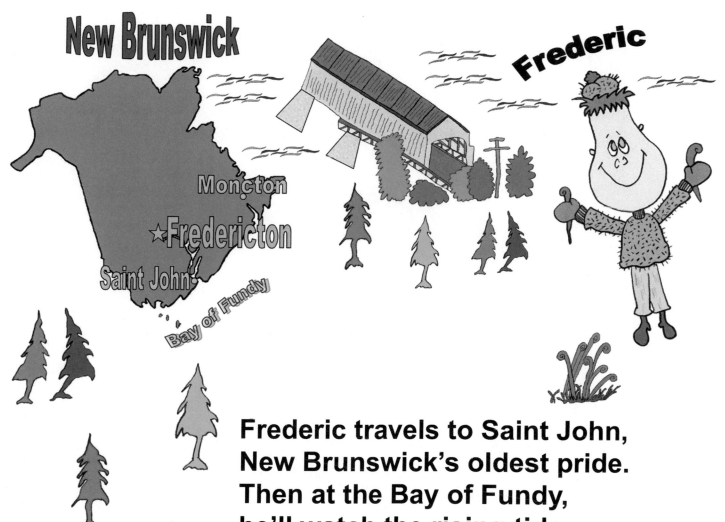

Frederic travels to Saint John,
New Brunswick's oldest pride.
Then at the Bay of Fundy,
he'll watch the rising tide.
He walks across the Hartland Bridge,
where Balsom firs he sees.
He munches on some fiddleheads
while hiking through the trees.

Nova Scotia

forestry/timber/paper

film/television

shellfish/lobster/fish

apples

blueberries

mining/coal

oil

N.S.

Andy next meets up with Halifax, who lives in Nova Scotia. Their first stop after Andy's arrival is the scenic and popular Cape Breton Island. Andy is amazed to learn that it is one of 3,800 islands in Nova Scotia! He and Halifax then take a trip to the Annapolis Valley to pick crisp, delicious apples and search for sweet, juicy blueberries. They finish Andy's visit with a journey to the coast of Nova Scotia, where Halifax helps his father catch lobsters. Halifax boasts to Andy that Nova Scotia is the world's largest exporter of lobsters.

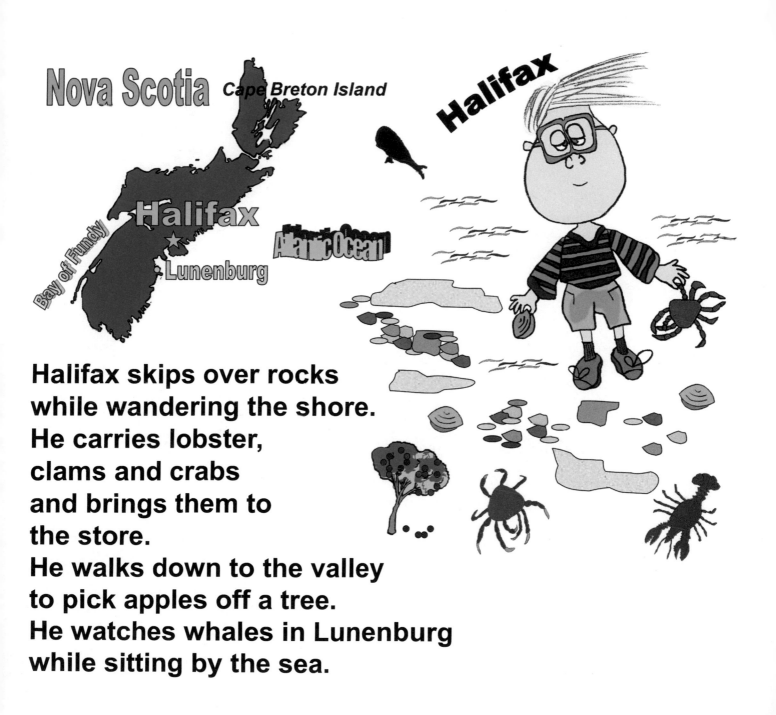

Nova Scotia   Cape Breton Island

Halifax

Bay of Fundy

Halifax
★
Lunenburg

Atlantic Ocean

Halifax skips over rocks
while wandering the shore.
He carries lobster,
clams and crabs
and brings them to
the store.
He walks down to the valley
to pick apples off a tree.
He watches whales in Lunenburg
while sitting by the sea.

Prince Edward Island

Andy's lovely friend, Charlotte, lives on Prince Edward Island, the smallest province in Canada. The Island was named after Prince Edward, who was the father of England's Queen Victoria. Most people living on Prince Edward Island have ancestors from Scotland or Ireland, and they make their living farming and growing vegetables. As the two tour the island, Andy is amazed at the sandstone cliffs, red dirt, and gorgeous sandy beaches. Charlotte points out patches of seaweed, or "Irish moss," along the way, and explains to Andy that it is used by the Islanders to thicken ice cream, cheese, and toothpaste.

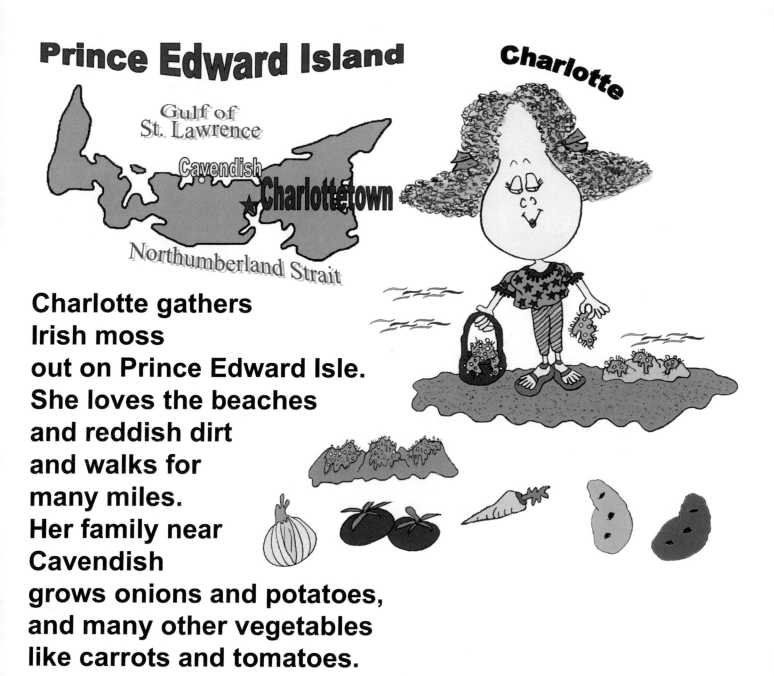

Prince Edward Island

Charlotte

Gulf of St. Lawrence

Cavendish

★ **Charlottetown**

Northumberland Strait

Charlotte gathers
Irish moss
out on Prince Edward Isle.
She loves the beaches
and reddish dirt
and walks for
many miles.
Her family near
Cavendish
grows onions and potatoes,
and many other vegetables
like carrots and tomatoes.

Newfoundland and Labrador

mining

forestry/timber

newsprint

hydro-electric

oil

lobster/fish

Andy's last visit is to Newfoundland and Labrador. In Newfoundland, he meets his friend, John, on a high cliff overlooking the icebergs in the Atlantic Ocean. This tall cliff is called "Signal Hill." John tells Andy the sad story of a large cruise ship, the "Titanic," which hit an iceberg and sank nearby Newfoundland many years ago. Andy looks out on the ocean from behind a telescope and looks for icebergs in the choppy waters. Afterward, John and Andy tour a steel mill that is owned by John's father, who proudly explains that Newfoundland produces the most iron ore and steel in all of Canada.

John stands very
proud and tall
on top of Signal Hill.
He looks out at the icebergs
on the ocean, calm and still.
He sees the lakes and forests,
with iron all around,
and views the islands, dunes, and hills,
high cliffs, and open ground.

This ends the journeys of Hiking Holly, Wandering Wally, and Ambling Andy. But feel free to take more trips with the three adventurous friends as they plot and plan to again travel All Across Canada!

FACEPAINT Nonprofit Books

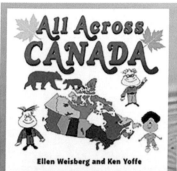

All Across CANADA
Ellen Weisberg and Ken Yoffe

All Across EUROPE
Ellen Weisberg and Ken Yoffe

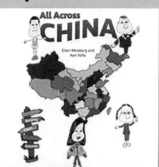

All Across CHINA
Ellen Weisberg and Ken Yoffe

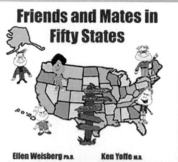

Friends and Mates in Fifty States
Ellen Weisberg Ph.D.   Ken Yoffe M.S.

Angel Rock Leap
Ellen Weisberg Ken Yoffe

What are microscopes?

FULL MOON

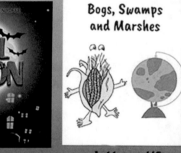

Bogs, Swamps and Marshes

GATHERING ROSES
ELLEN WEISBERG

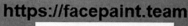

https://facepaint.team

Fruit of the Vine
Ellen Weisberg & Ken Yoffe

Making Emmie Smile
Ellen Weisberg & Ken Yoffe

FACEPAINT Nonprofit's multi-award-winning anti-bullying 3D animation, Justin and the Werloobee!

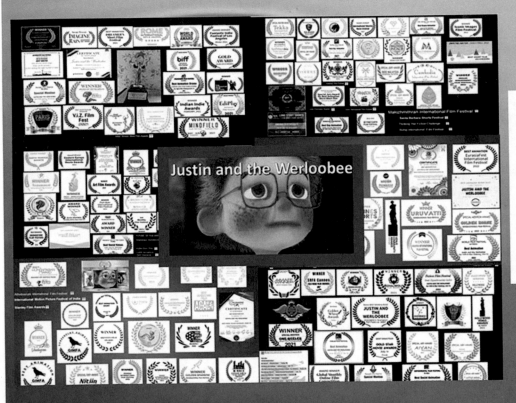

Watch on YouTube!